FIND HAPPII

THE
ELUSIVE
ONE

Stop Searching For Meaning
In The Wrong Places

Angel May

Table of Contents

Chapter 1:

Happy People Dream Big

Remember being a kid, and when somebody asked you what you wanted to be after growing up, you answered with a big dream: an astronaut, a ballerina, a scientist, a firefighter, or the President of the United States. You believed that you could achieve anything you set your mind at that no dream is too big that if you wanted, you would make it happen. But why is it that so many adults forget what it is like to dream big. Happy people are dreamers; if you want to become a happy person, you need to make dreaming big a habit; some people even say that if your dreams do not scare you, you are not dreaming big. Now you must be wondering how dreaming big can make you happy. Firstly, it helps you see that if you had a magic wand and you could get whatever you wanted, what you would want for yourself, and there is a chance that these dreams are things you want to achieve in your life somehow other. Secondly, it will help you in removing any fears you have about not being able to achieve your dreams because when you dream big, you think about what you want in your ideal world, and your fear will not come in your way because you would feel like you are living in that fantasy world. Lastly, you will put your dreams and desires into the universe, and the likelihood of making those dreams come true increases. Fulfilling your dreams makes you happy because you will be able to get what you have yearned for so long, and a sense of achievement will make you feel confident about yourself and the dream you had. Now you must have a question what should I do to start dreaming big I am going to outline some of the things you can practice!

Sit back, clear your mind and think about your desires and dreams. What do you want in life? If you had three wishes from a genie, what are the things you would ask for? What is something you would if no one was looking or if you weren't afraid. Now write these dreams down on a piece of paper. This way, they would seem more real. The next thing you should do is start reading some inspirational books that motivate you to start living your best life starting today! Lastly, make a list of goals you want to achieve and start working on them.

Chapter 2:

Happy People Do What Matters to Them

Think about what you want most out of life. What were you created for? What is your mission in life? What is your passion? You were put on this earth for a reason, and knowing that reason will help you determine your priorities.

I spent a total of four months in the hospital, healing from my sickness. During that time, I spent a lot of time thinking about my purpose in life. I discovered that my purpose is to help you change your lives by focusing on what matters most to you.

1. Create A Plan

Create a plan to get from where you are today to where you want to be. Maybe you need a new job. Maybe you need to go back to school. Maybe you need to deal with some relationship issues. Whatever it is, create a plan that will get you to where you want to be.

While I was in the hospital, I began to draft my life plan. My plan guides all of my actions, helps me focus on my relationships with my wife and daughter, and helps me keep working toward my life purpose. A life plan will help you focus your life too.

2. Focus On Now

Stop multitasking and focus on one thing at a time. It may be a project at work. It may be a conversation with your best friend. It may just be the book that you have wanted to read for months. The key is to focus on one thing at a time.

I plan each day the night before by picking the three most important tasks from my to-do list. In the morning, I focus on each one of these tasks individually until they are completed. Once I complete these three tasks, I check email, return phone calls, etc.

3. Just Say "No."

We all have too much to do and too little time. The only way you will find the time for the things that matter is to say "no" to the things that don't.

I use my purpose and life plan to make decisions about the projects and tasks I say yes to. If a project or task is not aligned with my purpose, a good fit with my life plan, and sometimes that I have time to accomplish, I say no to the project. Saying no to good opportunities gives you time to focus on the best opportunities.

Research tells us that 97 percent of people are living their life by default and not by design. They don't know where their life is headed and don't plan what they want to accomplish in life.

These steps will help you to decide what matters most to you. They will help you to begin living your life by design and not by default. Most importantly, they will help you to create a life focused on what matters to you.

Let me end by asking, "What matters most to you?

Chapter 3:

Do You Have to be Unhappy Now If You Want to be Successful Later?

Most of us, at some point or another, think that we will be happy once we achieve a particular goal. Society tells us that this is a good thing. We hear about athletes that are never satisfied until they have reached the top. We hear about entrepreneurs who worked like crazy to build a business that changed the world. The basic idea is that to be driven, you also have to be dissatisfied. Dissatisfied with second place. Dissatisfied with average. Then you have the other side of the equation: people who are happy with life as it is. They say that you need to develop the skill of "not wanting more." That you can be happy where you are right now. That you are already perfect.

Here's the problem: I want both. Maybe you do too. I like being happy. It's fun. I don't want to delay happiness until I reach some milestone. But I also like getting better. I don't want to settle for less than I can do in life. I'd like to be happy along the way and achieve my goals. For a long time, it bothered me that being happy (being satisfied) and being driven (being dissatisfied) seemed to be at odds with one another. I still don't have a lot of this figured out, but the more I study people who have had a great deal of success, the more I think that it's possible to be happy and driven.

Let's start with being driven. If you want to maximize your potential, then you will need to continue to work to become better both before and after you achieve a given goal. Why would someone do that? For example, if your goal was to make a million dollars and you made it, why would you keep working hard after that? The answer is a little more complicated than you might think.

In economics, there is a fundamental principle known as the Law of Diminishing Returns. Here's the short definition: as you get more of something, it becomes less valuable. This isn't just economic theory, a similar trend happens in real life. In other words, the goals and results that seem so valuable to you in the beginning actually become less valuable as you achieve more of them.

So, if the results mean less as you achieve more of them, how do you stay driven? By loving the practice of what you do. It's only the people who embrace their work as a craft and fall in love with the boredom of doing it day in and day out that stay driven over the long-term.

Guess what? This answer is now easy. If you love the practice of what you do, if you love the daily work, then you can be happy before and after you achieve your goals. When you learn to love the process of what you are doing and not focus so much on the goal, you automatically find happiness while staying driven. If you learn to love the practice of working out, then you'll be happy right now and you'll see results later. If you learn to love the practice of marketing your business, then you'll be happy right now and you'll see results later. If you learn to love the practice of supporting your friends and family, then you'll be happy now and see the results later. Happy and driven. Just one more reason why the system is better than the goal.

Chapter 4:

Happy People Are Busy But Not Rushed

Dan Pink points to an interesting new research finding — the happiest people are those that are very busy but don't feel rushed:

Who among us are the happiest? Newly published research suggests that fortunate folks have little or no excess time and yet seldom feel rushed.

This clicks with me. I love blogging, but I hate being under time pressure to get it done. This tension is very nicely demonstrated in a recent study by Hsee et al. (2010). When given a choice, participants preferred to do nothing unless given the tiniest possible reason to do something: a piece of candy. Then they sprang into action.

Not only did people only need the smallest inducement to keep busy, but they were also happier when doing something rather than nothing. It's as if people understand that being busy will keep them happier, but they need an excuse of some kind.

Having plenty of time gives you a feeling of control. Anything that increases your perception of control over a situation (whether it increases your control or not) can substantially decrease your stress level.

In Colorado, Steve Maier at the University of Boulder says that the degree of control that organisms can exert over something that creates stress determines whether the stressor alters the organism's functioning. His findings indicate that only uncontrollable stressors cause harmful effects. Inescapable or uncontrollable stress can be destructive, whereas the same stress that feels escapable is less destructive, significantly so...

Over and over, scientists see that the perception of control over a stressor alters the stressor's impact.

But heavy time pressure stresses you out and kills creativity. Low-to-moderate time pressure produces the best results.

If managers regularly set impossibly short time-frames or impossibly high workloads, employees become stressed, unhappy, and unmotivated—burned out. Yet, people hate being bored. It was rare for any participant in our study to report a day with very low time pressure, such days—when they did occur—were also not conducive to positive inner work life. In general, low-to-moderate time pressure seems optimal for sustaining positive thoughts, feelings, and drives.

Your reaction to being too busy and under time pressure might be to want to do nothing. But that can drop you into the bottom left corner.

And this makes you more unhappy than anything:

…**surveys "continue to show the least happy group to be those who quite often have excess time." Boredom, it seems, is burdensome.** So, stay busy—set goals. Challenge yourself, but make sure you have plenty of time to feel in control of the situation.

This is how games feel. And games are fun.

Chapter 5:

The High Cost of Good Intentions

Who has not experienced this before: We have been hurt and the person hurting us exclaims in a mixture of surprise and justification that they only meant well! The invocation of the good intention seems to them like an absolution of their responsibility for their action (or inaction) and thus our pain. Having worked as a psychotherapist for many years now with people on the receiving end of all kinds of well intentions (of parents, partners, siblings, classmates, teachers, religious leaders), it is clear to me that this not a sufficient ingredient for good outcome. Really, and I mean here even the truly well-intentioned efforts of some parents have at times caused havoc on the lives of their children, that it is heart wrenching to behold, how all sides have lost and suffered in these situations. Why is this so?

It seems that the good intentions may give some a sense of having fulfilled their aim already, thus preventing them to move to action. Like the good intention to ourselves to stop some bad habit of ours and paradoxically the more honest the intention meant at the time the more problematic it may turn out: it thus can better fulfil the very function of calming our worries and anxieties or doubts of being a bad parent, partner or person. Thus, good intentions can prove to ourselves that we are not the bad person we may fear we are. To give an example I am very familiar with is procrastinating to study for an exam by repeatedly telling myself, very seriously, that I am going to study "for real" first thing tomorrow, thus feeling at ease today and therefore being able to continue with my not-studying at that very moment, only to have the same pattern repeated the next day. It is the same pattern I see with people struggling with major dependency issues (of any substance and their often futile change efforts), who often will profess with great sincerity that they will stop. It calms them, and often their very afflicted family members as all can sense the honesty of the intent, but thus taking away the force that the suffering provides that is needed to overcome the problem. Good intentions thus can prevent action by removing the psychological motivation that is created by the normal self-doubt, concern about the future (exam, financial situation, you name it ...) or suffering that some undesired state creates, and thus turn against us or the people around us.

Then there is the situation where we do move to action, but it fails to meet the need of the recipient. I think this is captured well in the bible when Jesus talks about the ones on the right who have feed him when he was hungry, gave drink when he was thirsty. The gift matches the actual need of the recipient. But at times we give water when the person is hungry. This is especially confusing because the receiver may even feel an obligation to be thankful as the other went through the effort of bringing him a gift (albeit one he does not need)! I am not sure if it is possible to capture all the reasons this goes awry (still assuming truly good intentions), but what seems relevant is that the feedback about this mismatch does not reach the giver, for one because the recipient out of the above mentioned conflict does not give it. The second is that the giver will not hear or accept the signs and or direct feedback of the recipient. Why, because he meant well, which is sufficient in their minds to prove they are not the enemy and thus they can discount the other.

This is where tragedies start.

Chapter 6:

When It Is Time To Slow Down

Go faster. Do more. Hustle. Hustle even more. Sound familiar? Social media is full of influencers, entrepreneurs, and "gurus" touting the virtues of hustling at all costs. It's reached the point where hustling, and even just talking about hustling, appears to be more important that actually producing results. People confuse "hustling" with "productivity" and mistake "working" for "results." They don't have a mindfulness practice. They didn't make time for trips, fun, friends, or family. They think that if they worked harder, and worked more hours, they'd be more successful. That is not true if all you do is work, work. You will be burnt out.

The antidote to the "always hustling" mindset is "slowness." It sounds crazy, but slowing down can be the difference between success or failure, or between thriving and burning out. While more and more personal coaches and social-media influencers, qualified or not, tout the hustle lifestyle, successful leaders and entrepreneurs who actually create results in their lives know that slowing down builds the foundation for their success.

Here are four reasons why slowing down can actually help you accelerate your success, enjoy a deeper sense of fulfillment, and create the life you want.

1. What's the point of hustling if you're going in the wrong direction? Too many people work tirelessly down a path that won't give them the results they want. It's like running on a treadmill...you're working, but you're not going anywhere. Slow down and make time for clarity. You can't see where you're going if you're too busy running with your head down.

2. If your goal is to succeed, then you should be willing to take the time to honor what your mind, body, and spirit need to stay healthy. When every day provides 24 hours, there's really no excuse not to meditate, exercise, cook a healthy meal, or journal.

3. Too many people fail to see the benefits in their emotions. Emotions are a guide, and they help you take inventory of what's happening in and around you, and how best to respond. Successful people feel and manage their emotions, and they don't let them trigger bad behaviors or actions. There's a mantra that sums this up well: If you can name it, you can tame it. By slowing down, you can feel the emotions you're experiencing and describe them. In doing so, you can process them and let them guide you to a healthy response.

4. What good is hustling all the time if a single decision can undo all the work you invested? To put it simply, your mind is like a car engine: If you always have your pedal to the floor, the engine will redline, overheat, and fail. When you slow down and make time for rest and meditation, you lower your baseline for mental stress. When your mind isn't racing, it's free to absorb information, assess the circumstances, and make a good decision. If success requires making good decisions, and slowing down helps you make better decisions, then consider how you can invest more time in slowing down.

Consider the benefits described above and identify one simple step toward bringing more slowness into your life. See how that goes, and then try more. As someone who hustled himself into a concussion and changed, I can tell you that life is much better when you balance the hustle with slowness.

Chapter 7:

Five Ways To Control Your Thoughts

The power of thoughts.

Thoughts are very powerful because they greatly influence the direction our lives take. Our failures and successes are anchored on our thinking patterns. We score big in life when we learn how to dominate our minds and submit them to our desires.

The greater the external influence on our decisions, the more likely we lose control of our thoughts. Here are five ways to control your thoughts:

1. Meditation

It is the ability to reflect deeply on the occurrences in your life. Meditation is taking a deep reflective introspect of your life. Sometimes we need to take a break from our busy schedules and look back at the far we have come from. The journey we have walked hitherto shall inspire us to confidently move into the future.

Meditation is often perceived as old-fashioned because it is very basic. It appears unattractive but once you learn to do it in the right way, there is no turning back. Do not mistake it for idleness or wishful thinking because it is neither of them.

It begins with a mental walk down memory lane. You count your blessings one after another and take stock of your achievements. You can consolidate your thoughts through meditation as you plan for your next move. Meditation provides room for mental growth because you are free from any pressure to act therein.

2. Taking Feedback

How is feedback related to controlling our thoughts? There is a strong connection between the two. We live in a social world where interaction with different types of people is inevitable. Their perceptions and the doctrines they believe also vary. The people we live amongst are the mirror in which we can look at ourselves.

Strangers, friends, and family are very important circles that we surround ourselves with. Apart from strangers, our family and friends have been with us long enough to understand our thinking patterns. Their feedback about our decisions on various issues is very important because we can control our thoughts bordering on their suggestions.

We should learn to take feedback even from strangers we interact with briefly. They could make very important observations on our intellectuality which could spell the turning point of our thoughts. The power of feedback should not be underrated.

3. Taking a SWOT Analysis

We may have considered a SWOT analysis on our businesses but not on ourselves. If it is good for business, why is it not for ourselves? Our thoughts need to be audited from time to time for us to identify the red flags within. We can thereafter act from a point of knowledge because we understand our strengths and weaknesses even better.

We can work to improve our weaknesses and fortify our strengths in thoughts when we analyse them thoroughly. We can program our thoughts when we understand our personalities better.

A SWOT analysis enables us to identify the red zones we should not enter because they could spell doom for us. We also learn the limits we should not exceed because they threaten to disrupt our good thoughts. We operate within a healthy framework that our minds flourish.

4. Submitting To Spiritual Authority

It is good to subscribe to a belief or religion. Every religion has its practices that are beyond physical comprehension if your heart and thoughts are left out. The beauty of religious beliefs is its mystery in understanding the spirituality concepts around them.

Religion reinforces morality and upright thinking. Religious people train their thoughts within the confines of their beliefs. This enables them to be disciplined and control their thoughts not to stray away from the values they practice.

Religion rebukes evil thoughts and promotes the good ones. It is the prefect of upright thinking and curbs many evils before they even happen. If you have a problem with having your thoughts under control, consider joining a religion.

5. Consider the Fear of the Unknown

Fear is destructive when misused but very constructive when channelled correctly. The fear of the unknown is a limiting factor to very many things. Over the years, humanity has restrained itself from acting or thinking against acceptable societal norms because of the fear of the unknown that lies beyond.

You can bring your thoughts to submission when you consider the red zones that you should not approach, even in your mind. Your thinking will be disciplined not to stray into unchartered territories because of untold consequences.

In conclusion, controlling our thoughts is a big win if we at all want to be successful. These five ways are effective in bringing your thoughts to submission.

Chapter 8:

5 Ways To Set Life Goals

Having goals for things we want to do and working towards them is an important part of being human. The path towards our goals may not always run smoothly or be easy, but having goals, whether big or small, is part of what makes life good. It gives us a sense of meaning and purpose, points us in the direction we want to go and gets us interested and engaged, all of which are good for our overall happiness.

Over 2000 years ago, Aristotle said "Well begun is half done." And with regards to goals, he's right (as he seems to have been on a lot of things). Paying attention to how we set our goals makes us more like to achieve them and achieving them makes us feel good about ourselves and our lives.

1. Decide

Think of something you want to do or work towards. It doesn't matter what, as long as it's something you want to do - ideally something you're interested in or feel excited by. It should be something you want to do for its own sake not for something or someone else. It can be a big thing or a small thing - sometimes it is easier to get going with something small. And it often helps if it's something that's just a little bit beyond what you currently can do - goals that stretch us can be motivating!

2. Write it down Carefully

Writing down our goals increases our chances of sticking with them. Write down how you will know you have reached your goals and when you'd like to have achieved it by. Ask yourself: what it will 'look' like and how will you feel when you've done it? How does it connect to who or what you value in your life? Describe your goal in specific terms and timescales e.g. 'I want to plant lettuces, carrots and peas in the empty patch in my garden by the end of May' rather than 'I want to do some gardening.' Write your goals in terms of what you want, not what you don't want. For example: 'I want to be able to wear my favourite jeans again', rather than 'I don't want to be over-weight anymore'.

3. Tell someone

Telling someone we know about our goals also seems to increase the likelihood that we will stick at them.

4. Break your goal down

This is especially important for big goals. Think about the smaller goals that are steps on the way to achieving your bigger aim. Sometimes our big goals are a bit vague, like 'I want to be healthier'. Breaking these down helps us be more specific. So a smaller goal might be 'go running regularly' or even 'to be able to run around the park in 20 minutes without stopping'. Write down your smaller goals and try to set some dates to do these by too. Having several smaller goals makes each of them a bit easier and gives us a feeling of success along the way, which also makes it more likely that we'll stay on track towards our bigger goal.

5. Plan your first step

An ancient Chinese proverb says that the journey of 1000 miles starts with one step. Even if your goal isn't to walk 1000 miles, thinking about the first step on the way will really help to get you started. Even if you don't know where to start there's no excuse - your first step could be to research 'how to…' on the internet or think of people you could ask or to get a book on the subject from the library. Then think of your next step…and the next…

Keep going. Working towards our goals can sometimes be difficult and frustrating - so we need to persevere. If a step you're doing isn't working, think of something else you could try that still moves you forward, even a tiny bit. If you're struggling, ask people you know for their ideas on what you could do. They may help you see a different way. Thinking about different ways of reaching our goals makes it more likely we'll be successful. If you're really struck - take a break and then re-read the goal you wrote down when you started. If you need to adjust your goal - that's ok too. Then have another think about a small next step…

Celebrate. When you reach your goal take time to enjoy it and thank those that helped you. Think about what you enjoyed and learned along the way. Now, what is your next goal or project going to be?

Chapter 9:

Why Nobody Cares When You Fail?

In a world this big, it is hard for everyone to care about others. We all have a busy life; we have thousands of things to do before we go to bed. Everybody focuses on themselves and is trying to make their life better. So when anyone around us wins, their success makes the noise, and people notice that. Like when you sit in an interview, nobody will see how many times you have failed, but they will see that there is a reason that you are sitting in that interview.

The main reason why nobody cares if you fail is that everyone has a life of their own, and they can't just think or care about your failure for your whole life; sure, they would try to comfort you, but eventually, they will have to go back to their own lives, and they wouldn't care about your failure anymore, now they can't be blamed for this because it is simply human nature to resume their own lives.

People don't care about your failure, I mean, of course, your family and friends would, but others wouldn't because failures don't excite them; however insensitive it may sound to you, but it is the truth. People prefer to listen to success stories that excite them and, above all, motivate them.

The people themselves need someone to give them hope that one day they can also become a success, but nobody wants to care about failures; they would rather care about your success, so don't give up just yet because if they don't care now, they will care later. "Life is hard" we all have heard this, but this hits differently when we fail, but failures are not something to be afraid of; in this life, you can't always win; sometimes, you need to fail to gain success.

And honestly, what can people even do if you fail? Nobody can give you a happy and good life, and only you can make yourself a success. Failing is not a bad thing; it is something that no one can avoid, so when you fail, and you think that nobody cares, think for a second that maybe these people have also been through the same, and they know how it feels when people acknowledge your failures. People prefer to have a person they can call a hero, and they like to hear the stories of that hero and his success; even when the hero fails, nobody cares about his failure because they prefer to mind their own business when something like that happens.

Everyone is too focused on their own life, their own goals, and their failures to care about someone else's failures because they would rather care about their lives than yours, so don't take it negatively; it is okay if they don't care, use that to your advantage and work on yourself, now is the time to work hard and be successful and once your successful everyone will care.

The only thing you can do is forget about the people and remember yourself, remember that everyone who is a hero now has failed more than twice, so don't go thinking why they don't care because everyone has problems that they are worried about now and that is the reason they don't care. The only thing you should remember is that you should never give up because "Success comes from failures."

Chapter 10:

10 Signs You've Outgrown Your Life

Growth can be hard, but it is necessary sometimes you outgrow your life, and understandably it is the scar you are required to stretch yourself to something you haven't been familiar with. Growth demands you to take risks and leave your comfort behind. Another important aspect is that you should be vulnerable because whenever there is growth, failure is there. Leaving your old life behind is scary, but the alternative to that is even scarier because staying in the same position for a long time can be soul-crushing.

Here are ten signs that you have outgrown your life

1. You Can No Longer Relate To The People Around You

When you realize that you are surrounded by people you have nothing to talk about, it's an obvious sign that you have outgrown them. There is also a chance that you stop enjoying the activities you previously participated in and enjoyed with them, plus communication feels like a struggle. You will receive comments from your close circle that you have changed, and you won't exactly be happy with those comments but be prepared. Others telling you that you have changed should be considered a compliment. It simply means you're growing.

2. Everyone Around You Is Changing

Another sign of you outgrowing your life is that everyone around you is changing as well. If your friends and family are making all kinds of changes in their lives and you're sitting alone on some barstool, it's time to take inventory of your life. You have outgrown your old life, so now it's time to set some new goals.

3. You Have A Constant Feeling of Discontent

Constant dissatisfaction when you were previously content with the same circumstances is a huge sign of outgrowing your life. The reason could be your current life doesn't challenge you the way it once did, and when life isn't challenging, it becomes mundane, and depression creeps in. Living in discontentment is not a way to live. You should listen to your inner voice and make some changes.

4. You're Interested In Different Things

Being interested in different activities that you previously found boring and they vastly deviate from what you found interesting that simply means you are outgrowing your current life. You should follow this inclination and engage yourself in new things. It will keep your life fresh and exciting!

5. You Fantasize About Having A Different Life

Constantly dreaming about how you wish your life was a sure sign. If you were obsessed with your life, you wouldn't be consistently envisioning a different one.

Maybe you think about living in a new city, having a new job, having different relationships, and/or new hobbies.

Recognize that you've outgrown your life and make those fantasies a reality!

6. You Have New Goals That Are Vastly Different Than Your Life

Having goals and working toward them is one of the healthiest things you can do for yourself!

BUT if your new goals would change the course of your life, you've likely outgrown your life.

7. You're Bored With Your Life

You might be bored with your job or career. Maybe you're bored with your relationships and the activities you used to love.

If your days feel dull, you're ready to shake your life up!

It's one thing to feel bored here and there but being bored EVERY DAY of your life is an awful way to live and a glaringly huge sign you've outgrown your life!

8. You Feel Like You're Going Through the Motions

This is a BIG sign you've started to outgrow your life.

If you wake up every day with zero enthusiasm and move throughout the day on autopilot, you're ready for huge life changes.

I've had points in my life where I was just getting through the day simply existing. It's a depressing way to live.

Don't accept a mundane life for yourself. Make the changes necessary to get excited about your days!

9. You Start Trying To Fill A Void

Maybe you're doing it with shopping, food, alcohol, sex, etc. This one can be hard to identify because you might just think you lack discipline or control.

Take inventory of the thoughts you have when you're tempted to engage in your addiction. Are you trying to numb feelings of dissatisfaction with your life?

10. Your Vision Board Is 100% Unrelated to Any Part of Your Current Life

This was a HUGE eye-opener for me. When I created my vision board in the New Year, it was different from my life. I have since begun to take steps to make my vision board my reality.

What does your vision board look like? Is it different than your current life? If so, you've likely outgrown your life.

What can you do to start making your vision board a reality?

Chapter 11:

Consistency Can Bring You Happiness

Happiness is an individual concept.

One man's riches are another man's rubbish.

As humans we are not happy if we do not have a routine, a reason to get up, and a purpose to live.

Without working towards something consistently, we become lost.

We begin to drift.

Drifting with no purpose eventually leads to emptiness.

When we are drifting in a job we hate,

We are trading our future away,

When we inconsistent in our relationships,

Problems are bound to arise.

Choose consistent focus instead.

Figure out exactly what you want and start to change it.

Employ consistent routines and habits that to move you towards your goals.

Consistency and persistence are key to success and happiness.

Without consistent disciplined effort towards what we want, we resign to a life of mediocrity.

Read a book for an hour consistently every single day.

You will become a national expert in 1 year.

In 5 years, a global expert.

That is the power of consistency.

Instead, people spend most of their free time scrolling through social media.

Consistency starts in the mind.

Control your thoughts to be positive despite the circumstances.

Nothing in the world can make us happy if we choose not to be.

Choose to be happy now and consistently working towards your goals.

We cannot be happy and successful if we dwell in the day to day setbacks.

We must consistently move like a bulldozer.

We have to keep going no matter what.

Nothing stays in the path of a bulldozer for too long.

In life, no matter where you are, you only ever have two choices.

Choose to stay where you are? Or choose to keep moving?

If where you are is making you happy, then by all means do more of it.

If not. What will? And why?

This should be clear before you take action.

Start with the end in your mind.

Let your body catch-up to it afterwards.

The end result is your what.

The action required is your how.

Concentrate on the what and the how and it will all be revealed soon enough.

Concentrate consistently on what you want for yourself and your family.

Distraction and lack of consistent action is a killer of happiness and success.

Your happiness is the life you want.

Take consistent action towards that life you've always dreamed of.

Commitment and endurance is part of that process.

On earth things need time to nurture and grow.

Everything in life depends on it.

The right conditions for maximum growth.

You can't just throw a seed on the concrete and expect it to grow with no soil and water,

Just as you can't simply wish for change and not create the right environment for success.

A seed requires not just consistent sunlight,

But the perfect combination of water and nutrients as well.

You might have given that seed sunlight,

just as you have your dream hope,

But without faith and consistent action towards the goal, nothing will happen.

The seed will still stay a seed forever.

Consistency in thought and action is everything towards happiness.

Nothing can grow without it.

Your success can be measured by your time spent working towards your goals.

If we consistently do nothing, we become successful in nothing.

If we have to do something, should it not be something worth doing?

Start doing things that make you happy and fulfilled.

Consistency towards something that makes you happy is key towards lasting success.

Adapt when necessary but remain consistent with the end result in mind.

The path can be changed, when necessary, but the destination cannot.

Accepting anything less is admitting defeat.

Consistent concentration on the end result can and will be tested.

It however cannot be defeated, unless you quit.

If we remain steadfast in our belief that this is possible for us, it will be possible.

After a while things will seem probable. Eventually it becomes definite.

Continue to believe you can do it despite the circumstances.

Continue despite everyone around you saying you can't do it.

In spite of social status,

in spite of illness or disability,

in spite of age, race or nationality,

know you can do nearly anything if you consistently put all of your mind

and body towards the task.

Take the pressure off.

There is no set guideline.

It is what you make of it.

There is no set destination or requirements.

Those are set my you.

The only competition is yourself from yesterday.

If you can consistently outperform that person, your success is

guaranteed.

Consistent concentration and action towards your dream is key you your

success and happiness.

Chapter 12:

7 Crucial Life Skills to Have

Life skills is a term used to describe many of your abilities to deal effectively with everyday problems. Whether it's problem-solving, learning decision-making, or acquiring communication skills, life skills expand your thinking and can be helpful in both your personal and professional endeavours

Here are some essential life skills that everyone should learn and master, regardless of age, gender, location, or situation.

1. Creativity

Creativity is considered one of the essential life skills you can possess. Creativity helps you better solve problems and allows you to see things from a different perspective. Thinking creatively in your personal life or at work can help you think outside the box, come up with fresh ideas and strategies, and better deal with uncertainty.

Other benefits of creativity include:

1. You can express yourself candidly and honestly.
2. Reduce stress and anxiety.

3. Give a sense of purpose.

4. Improving thinking and problem-solving skills.

5. It makes you feel proud and accomplished.

2. Problem-Solving

Another helpful life skill to learn and master is problem-solving. Addressing issues that matter to organizations and individuals puts you in control of your environment. Identifying and fixing the root cause of the problem can bring you great satisfaction and success. As you face and overcome many obstacles in your lifetime, troubleshooting can help you:

1. Tests your ability to analyze information and evaluate situations.

2. Propose new strategies to solve problems.

3. Increase your self-esteem and ability level.

3. Communication

Effective communication is a life skill that will take you far, both personally and professionally. You'll meet people from all walks of life throughout your life, so knowing how to be actively involved can help strengthen relationships, increase productivity, and build trust. Other benefits of communication skills include:

1. Improving Relationships at Work.
2. It helps you stay organized.
3. Boost self-esteem.
4. It enables you to create a successful family.
5. Providing opportunities to participate in community life.

4. Leadership

Understanding the power and value of leadership is an essential lifelong learning skill that can profoundly impact the lives of others. Leaders not only have control, they know how to motivate, inspire and empower others. To be a successful leader, you need to teach them to see the strengths of others and to believe in their worth. Leadership can benefit all areas of your life by helping you:

1. Strengthening communication skills.
2. Character development.
3. Build trust.

Leadership skills can be acquired through experience and education.

5. Critical Thinking

Learning to think critically is critical to future success. Responsible, productive, and independent thinking can help in all areas of life.

Thinking systematically helps improve the way you express your thoughts and ideas. Some of the essential benefits of critical thinking are:

1. It helps you make better decisions.
2. Make you happier.
3. Better relationship.

Make sure your comments are educated and well informed. Critical thinking also transcends cultural norms and is open to those around you, helping you learn and understand other factors that can influence the decisions of others.

6. Self Awareness

Self-awareness refers to recognizing or recognizing emotions, beliefs, behaviours, and motivations, among other traits, including strengths and weaknesses. Self-awareness is an essential life skill because it allows us to understand better who we are, how we feel, and what makes us unique and different from others. By becoming self-aware, you can make lifestyle changes that will help you think more positively. Here are some key benefits of self-awareness:

1. Increased communication.
2. Rich emotional intelligence.
3. Improve your listening and empathy skills.
4. Improving Leadership and Opportunities.

7. Empathy

In addition to being assertive, it is imperative to empathize with the people around you. Understanding the feelings of others and showing compassion and support can help us respond appropriately. Whether hanging out with a loved one or showing interest in someone at work, empathy can build trust and eliminate conflicts with others.

Along with interpersonal and challenging skills, life skills are essential, and we cannot deny it. The impact of learning skills on your life is enormous. There are several life skills. In this article, I have mentioned some essential life skills that must be learned.

Chapter 13:

How Volunteering Can Make You Happy

With busy lives, it can be hard to find time to volunteer. However, the benefits of volunteering can be enormous. Volunteering offers vital help to people in need, worthwhile causes, and the community, but the benefits can be even greater for you, the volunteer. The right match can help you to find friends, connect with the community, learn new skills, and even advance your career.

Giving to others can also help protect your mental and physical health. It can reduce stress, combat depression, keep you mentally stimulated, and provide a sense of purpose. While it's true that the more you volunteer, the more benefits you'll experience, volunteering doesn't have to involve a long-term commitment or take a huge amount of time out of your busy day. Giving in even simple ways can help those in need and improve your health and happiness.

One of the more well-known benefits of volunteering is the impact on the community. Volunteering allows you to connect to your community and make it a better place. Even helping out with the smallest tasks can make a real difference to the lives of people, animals, and organizations in need. And volunteering is a two-way street: It can benefit you and your family as much as the cause you choose to help. Dedicating your time as a volunteer helps you make new friends, expand your network, and boost your social skills.

One of the best ways to make new friends and strengthen existing relationships is to commit to a shared activity together. Volunteering is a great way to meet new people, especially if you are new to an area. It strengthens your ties to the community and broadens your support network, exposing you to people with common interests, neighbourhood resources, and fun and fulfilling activities.

While some people are naturally outgoing, others are shy and have a hard time meeting new people. Volunteering gives you the opportunity to practice and develop your social skills, since you are meeting regularly with a group of people with common interests. Once you have momentum, it's easier to branch out and make more friends and contacts.

Volunteering Helps Counteract the Effects of Stress, Anger, and Anxiety

The social contact aspect of helping and working with others can have a profound effect on your overall psychological well-being. Nothing relieves stress better than a meaningful connection to another person. Working with pets and other animals has also been shown to improve mood and reduce stress and anxiety.

Volunteering Combats Depression

Volunteering keeps you in regular contact with others and helps you develop a solid support system, which in turn protects you against depression.

Volunteering Makes You Happy

By measuring hormones and brain activity, researchers have discovered that being helpful to others delivers immense pleasure. Human beings are hard-wired to give to others. The more we give, the happier we feel.

Chapter 14:

How To Succeed In Life Before Quitting

Getting rid of a job is always risky, especially if you want to succeed in life. Sometimes we have to choose our satisfactory activity even if we are settled for something else. But you have to keep in mind that these risks might be worth pursuing your dreams. You should have confidence in yourself if you are letting go of your stable job. You are starting by taking small baby steps and keeping a clear idea in your mind of what you want or if quitting your job is the right decision.

When wanting to quit a full-time job, you need to make sure of some things first. One of them is financial stability. It's not something you can leave on its own. Taking care of your finances should be your first step as it will help you in further needs. Try not to ask for help much. Make yourself capable of purchasing your needs and wants.

To be a successful person, the most important thing is not to be afraid of failure. You have to plant courage and confidence in your mind. Quitting will be easier when you know what you are doing. It keeps you aware of your needs and makes your decision stronger. You cannot second guess yourself if you make the right choice. Be willing to fail ever once in a while.

Positivity in life is an easier way to be successful. Take everything lightly and make sure that negativity gets ignored. You cannot get discouraged if people don't support your ideas and goals. Suppose you feel like you should quit. Go for it. The world will not see the journey, but the results will be visualized clearly for them. So, keep positivity in your mind and heart.

Becoming a successful person comes with a lot to take in, and it might not be as easy as it will have seemed. So, the smartest move that anyone can make is to take their time while making any decision in this regard. So should weigh all of your options while keeping your mental and physical health in check. Choose the best one for yourself always.

You should be ready for anything that comes your way. Don't be scared of rejection. Don't be scared of others' opinions. Even ask for advice from someone if you need help in deciding. Ask your superiors for guidance in this regard. Let people motivate you for a greater cause. And better, motivate yourself. The secret to success is to enjoy your work. If you work thinking that you will earn only or become powerful only, you are wrong. You will be stuck in one place for a long time. You need to make sure to have fun along the way. That way, everything you do will be worth it.

Becoming successful before quitting can be quite challenging, but that is one way to become yourself. You are getting a focused view of what you want in life and how you'll work things out. Just make sure to have all the right ingredients you'll need to quit one part of your life to start a new one. And hopefully a better part of your life for yourself.

Chapter 15:

What To Do When You Feel Like Your Work is not Good Enough

Feeling like your work is not good enough is very common; your nerves can get better of you at any time throughout your professional life. There is nothing wrong with nerves; It tells you that you care about improving and doing well. Unfortunately, too much nervousness can lead to major self-doubt, and that can be crippling. You are probably very good at your work, and when even once you take a dip, you think that things are not like how they seem to you. If this is something you're feeling, then you're not alone, and this thing is known as Imposter Syndrome. This term is used to describe self-doubt and inadequacy. This one thing leaves people fearing that there might be someone who will expose them. The more pressure you apply to yourself, the more dislocation is likely to occur. You create more anxiety, which creates more fear, which creates more self-doubt. You don't have to continue like this. You can counter it.

Beyond Work

If your imposter syndrome affects you at work, you should take some time out and start focusing on other areas of your life. There are chances that there is something in your personal life that is hindering your work life. This could be anything your sleep routine, friends, diet, or even your relationships. There is a host of external factors that can affect your performance. If there are some boxes you aren't ticking, then there is a high chance of you not performing well at work.

You're Better Than You Think

When you're being crippled by self-doubt, the first thing you have to think about is why you were hired in the first place. The interviewers saw something in you that they believed would improve the business.

So, do you think they would recruit someone who can't do the job? No, they saw your talent, they saw something in you, and you will come good.

When you find yourself in this position, take a moment to write down a few things that you believe led to you being in the role you are now. What did those recruiters see? What did your boss recognize in you? You can also look back on a period of time where you were clicking and felt victorious. What was different then versus now? Was there an external issue like diet, exercise, socializing, etc.?

Check Yourself Before You Wreck Yourself

A checklist might be of some use to you. If you have a list to measure yourself against, then it gives you more than just one thing to judge yourself against. We're far too quick to doubt ourselves and criticize harshly.

The most obvious checklist in terms of work is technical or hard skills, but soft skills matter, too. It's also important to remember that while you're technically proficient now, things move quickly, and you'll reach a point where everything changes, and you have to keep up. You might not ever excel at something, but you can accept the change and adapt to the best of your ability.

It matters that you're hard-working, loyal, honest, and trustworthy. There's more to judge yourself on than just your job. Even if you make a mistake, it's temporary, and you can fix it.

Do you take criticism well? Are you teachable? Easy to coach? Soft skills count for something, which you can look to even at your lowest point and recognize you have strengths.

When you're struggling through a day, week, or even a month, take one large step backward and think about what it is you're unhappy with. What's causing your unhappiness, and how can you improve it?

It comes down to how well you know yourself. If you're clear on what your values are and what you want out of life, then you're going to be fine. If the organization you work for can't respect your values and harness your strengths, then you're better off elsewhere. So, it is extremely important to take time out for that self-check-in there could be times you talk to yourself in negative light. Checking in with yourself regularly and not feeding yourself negativity could be one-step forward.

Chapter 16:

How to Face Difficulties in Life

Have you noticed that difficulties in life come in gangs attacking you when you're least prepared for them? The effect is like being forced to endure an unrelenting nuclear attack.

Overcoming obstacles in life is hard. But life is full of personal challenges, and we have to summon the courage to face them. These test our emotional mettle — injury, illness, unemployment, grief, divorce, death, or even a new venture with an unknown future.

Here are some strategies to help carry you through:

1. Turn Toward Reality

So often, we turn away from life rather than toward it. We are masters of avoidance! But if we want to be present—to enjoy life and be more effective in it—we must orient ourselves toward facing reality. When guided by the reality principle, we develop a deeper capacity to deal with life more effectively. What once was difficult is now easier. What once frightened us now feels familiar. Life becomes more manageable. And there's something even deeper that we gain: Because we can see that we have grown stronger, we have greater confidence that we can grow even stronger still.

This is the basis of feeling capable, which is the wellspring of a satisfying life.

2. Embrace Your Life as It Is Rather Than as You Wish It to Be

The Buddha taught that the secret to life is to want what you have and do not want what you don't have. Being present means being present to the life that you have right here, right now. There is freedom in taking life as it comes to us—the good with the bad, the wonderful with the tragic, the love with the loss, and the life with the death. When we embrace it all, then we have a real chance to enjoy life, value our experiences, and mine the treasures that are there for the taking. When we surrender to the reality of who we are, we give ourselves a chance to do what we can do.

3. Take Your Time

As the story of the tortoise and the hare tells us, slow and steady wins the race. By being in a hurry, we actually thwart our own success. We get ahead of ourselves. We make more mistakes. We cut corners and pay for them later. We may learn the easy way but not necessarily the best way. As an old adage puts it: The slower you go, the sooner you get there. Slow, disciplined, incremental growth is the kind of approach that leads to lasting change.

Chapter 17:

How To Simplify Your Life And Maximise Your Results

The word "simplicity" seems almost like a single-word oxymoron. The fast-paced, tech-driven world we live in makes it almost impossible to keep it simple. More and more apps are created every day to help make daily tasks such as communicating, shopping, and budgeting simpler – but the truth is, life these days couldn't be more complex.

We can agree that on most days, 24 hours just isn't enough time to get it all done, even though our multi-tasking skills are at their max. There is a widespread need for a simpler routine, but achieving success where that's concerned, is complicated. Where do you even start? (See, even the first step is hard!)

The Pareto principle, commonly known as the 80/20 rule, is a rule that has been universally accepted to explain the balance of output vs. input. The 80/20 rule states that 80% of results come from 20% of the action in a simple sentence. The 80/20 rule has proven to be true time and time again in many aspects of business such as economics, sales, real estate, health and safety, information technology, and sports.

How does this apply to you? It boils down to 80% of overall output -or- your accomplishments, at home, at work, in the gym, etc., comes from 20% of input -or- focused time, energy, and effort. So, in other words, to make the simplest and most effective strides to your goals, you have to focus on the right 20%. Clear as mud? Okay, let's look at an example. Have you ever known someone who tends to keep busy all the time but never really gets anything accomplished? That is because they are taking the path of least resistance, working on lots of little things that don't have a high value or return. Prioritizing quick, trivial, or less effective tasks over more difficult, time-consuming, yet impactful tasks is the procrastination paradox that leads to running in circles but never getting things done.

What's the solution? Goal prioritization and time management. Try this exercise to help simplify your goal and task list down to what matters to you.

1. Make a list of 10 things you want to accomplish in the next 30 days – in no particular order. These ten goals can apply to any area of your life – personal or professional. (The first of a new month is a great time to try this for the first time.)

2. Assign a category to each goal – family/friends, career, personal, etc.

3. Review the list carefully, considering the areas of your life each goal will impact. Now rank these 10 goals from 1-10; 1 = most important, 10 = least important.

If you are going to take Bruce Lee's path to simplicity by "hacking away at the unessential," – first determine what is essential (AKA rank your goals and priorities) and then start to remove the small barriers in your path that you can control.

Chapter 18:

Why Considering Therapy Could Be An Option

Telling someone they should go to therapy or that they need therapy can be stigmatizing. It may be difficult to watch a loved one deal with mental health challenges, but it's important for people to choose to seek help on their own—as long as they aren't putting themselves or anyone else in danger.

Encouraging someone you care about to look into possible therapy options, even offering to review potential therapists with them, is generally a better way to show support. People who feel forced into therapy may feel resistant and find it harder to put in the work needed to make change.

While therapy can help people work through issues that lead to thoughts of suicide, it's usually not the best option for people in crisis. If you are in crisis, you can get help right away by reaching out to a suicide helpline through phone, text message, or online chat. You may be encouraged to call or visit the nearest emergency room. A therapist can help support you going forward, once you are no longer in crisis.

When any type of mental health or emotional concern affects daily life and function, therapy may be recommended. Therapy can help you learn about what you're feeling, why you might be feeling it, and how to cope.

Therapy also offers a safe place to talk through life challenges such as breakups, grief, parenting difficulties, or family struggles. For example, couples counselling can help you and your partner work through relationship troubles and learn new ways of relating to each other. Note that crisis resources, not couples counselling, are typically recommended for abusive relationships.

It may take some consideration before you decide you're ready for therapy. You might want to wait and see if time, lifestyle changes, or the support of friends and family improves whatever you're struggling with.

If you experience any of the following emotions or feelings to the extent that they interfere with life, therapy may help you reduce their effects. It's especially important to consider getting help if you feel controlled by symptoms or if they could cause harm to yourself or others.

1. Overwhelm

You might feel like you have too many things to do or too many issues to cope with. You might feel like you can't rest or even breathe. Stress and overwhelm can lead to serious physical health concerns.

2. Fatigue

This physical symptom often results from or accompanies mental health issues. It can indicate depression. Fatigue can cause you to sleep more than usual or have trouble getting out of bed in the morning.

3. Disproportionate Rage, Anger, or Resentment

Everyone feels angry at times. Even passing rage isn't necessarily harmful. Seeking support to deal with these feelings may be a good idea when they don't pass, are extreme compared to the situation, or if they lead you to take violent or potentially harmful actions.

Chapter 19:

How To Stop Worrying and Go To Sleep

Have trouble falling asleep, staying asleep or just feeling rested? The bad news is that it may be due to personal lifestyle habits. However, the good news is that those are easy to change to help get you on your way to sleeping better. Some people lay in bed staring at the ceiling in part due to chronic pain, depression, medications, or other substances that can interfere with sleep. When you treat those issues, often it will naturally help improve your ability to sleep.

However, despite addressing other medical or psychiatric conditions, sleep difficulties often will persist. People who have chronic insomnia worry excessively about sleep and the effects of insomnia. They also become more and more agitated and tense as bedtime gets closer. If you're very worried about getting good sleep, you can put a lot of effort into getting sleep and have a lot of anxiety at night. This makes you more alert and can keep you lying in bed wide awake.

We are offering some suggestions that can help improve your sleep habits, including individuals who suffer from chronic insomnia. Trying to break some of the patterns that you may have developed is often the key.

Keep Your Sleep Schedule The Same

You can improve your sleep by ensuring that you have a consistent sleep schedule. Avoid staying up late on weekends and sleeping in, then trying to go to bed at your regular time on Sunday night. We call it social jet lag because it's like you've flown to California, and now you're trying to adjust back to the time zone difference. So, keep those times as consistent as you can." Going to bed early or sleeping in to catch up only leads to more fragmented and poor quality sleep. Typically, you go to bed two hours early and then just lay there wide awake, continuing to associate your bed with not sleeping.

Take Some Quiet Time Before Bedtime

Quiet time is worth its weight in gold. Give yourself at least 30 to 60 minutes of quiet, relaxed time before bed as a buffer. Nix phone screen time and replace it with reading a book, listening to calming music, taking a warm bath, or having some decaffeinated herbal tea.

Distract Yourself If You Can't Sleep

If you can't fall asleep, get up and try to restart by doing something to distract yourself before going back to bed. It could be flipping through magazines; calming yoga stretches or some type of relaxing hobby like knitting or colouring. Avoid anything that's goal-directed or too physically or mentally activating such as house chores, paying bills or working on a computer. While it may be tempting to grab your phone off your nightstand and scroll endlessly through social media, don't. The blue light emitted from your phone or tablet screen can inhibit your natural melatonin production which is a hormone that is involved in the timing of our internal circadian sleep clock.

Learn How To Relax

Learning relaxation techniques such as meditation, guided imagery and progressive muscle relaxation can go a long way in helping you fall asleep. A sleep specialist can help you learn this as well as ways to calm your mind and your muscles and reduce or eliminate all the racing thoughts and worries. Dealing with stress in a healthy way is important for not only sleep, but your overall health, too. "Practice the relaxation techniques and develop them as a skill during the day when you feel good and are already calm, rather than trying to do them for the first time at bedtime,"

Keep a Sleep Log

Think of this as the adult sister to that diary you've kept in middle school. You can track the details of your sleep patterns and lifestyle habits. This can help you see trends in your behaviour and will be useful when you discuss your insomnia with your doctor or a sleep disorder specialist. If writing things down the old-fashioned way isn't your jam, try smartphone apps or your smartwatch to help you keep a log.

Chapter 20:

Mental Health Workbook For Depression

Mental illness affects 19% of the adult population, 46% of adolescents and 13% of children each year. People with mental health problems may be in the family, live in the neighbourhood, teach children, work in an adjacent building, or sit in the same seat.

However, only half of those affected receive treatment, often due to mental health stigma. Untreated mental illness can increase health care costs, reduce academic and work performance, reduce employment opportunities, and increase suicide risk.

Mental illness is a physical illness of the brain that causes disturbances in thinking, behavior, energy, or emotions that make it challenging to meet the needs of ordinary life. We are beginning to unravel the complex causes of these diseases, including genetics, brain chemistry, brain structure, trauma and other medical conditions such as heart disease. Stigma affects the number of people seeking treatment and the number of resources available for appropriate treatment. Stigma and misinformation can seem like insurmountable obstacles to people with mental illness. Here are some powerful methods that can help.

1. Negative Thoughts and Depression

Anxiety or negative thoughts are common in people with depression. It affects your ability to focus on doing better and makes you more susceptible to unhealthy emotions.

Here are some tips to help you control your anxiety and reduce negative thoughts.

- Write down your concerns.
- Ponder each problem and consider how realistic the negative thoughts are.
- Explore alternative ideas and explanations.
- Try not to focus on the things you cannot change.
- Focus on the present.
- Accept your thoughts without getting involved in them.
- Write down the problem and brainstorm.
- Write down the pros and cons of each option and choose the one that seems most appropriate.
- See if that solves the problem.
- Avoid making important decisions in your life during this period.

2. Sleeping Patterns and Depression

Depression can interfere with your sleep patterns. To fully recover, it is crucial to restore a typical sleep pattern. Here are some tips for a good night's sleep.

- Try to go to bed and wake up at about the same time each day.
- If you're worried about work at night, set aside time during the day to solve problems. Avoid caffeinated beverages after 4 pm and avoid drinking more than two cups of caffeinated drinks (such as coffee, strong tea, cola, or energy drinks) per day. Avoid alcohol to help you sleep better. Alcohol breaks down in your body, making you sleepless and waking up more often.
- Take a break before going to bed.
- If you are working or studying, stop and do something relaxing for at least 30 minutes before bed.
- Avoid online activities such as social media for an hour before bed and leave your phone in your bedroom and other rooms at night.

3. Staying Active

When you are depressed, you may not enjoy activities you once enjoyed. You may also think you won't like something, but you want it more than you expect when you do. If you don't try, the number of things that will

73

help you cope with depression will decrease. To increase the number of activities you enjoy, you can:

- List all actions you have enjoyed before - including as many as possible.
- Schedule one of these activities every day.
- Increase the amount of time you have available for activities you enjoy.
- After school, think or write down what you like about it.
- Talk to others about activities they enjoy.
- Keeping walking will help you get better.
- The more you recover, the more you can enjoy the action.

4. Dealing with Irritability

Some people with depression may feel irritable. These feelings can be exacerbated by changes in your sleep patterns and lifestyle.
HELP MAKE IT ON YOUR OWN:

- Talk to friends, family, and co-workers about how you feel and what makes you irritable.
- If you are angry, stop and take time to calm down.
- Take regular breaks to reduce the effects of irritating or irritating situations
- Talk to people who support you.

- Many people with depression may experience anxiety at the same time.

In most cases, treating anxiety is similar to treating depression. Still, it's essential to talk to your doctor or mental health professional about your anxiety symptoms so they can treat both conditions.

Depression can be temporary or long-term. Treatment does not always completely cure depression. However, with treatment, symptoms can often be better managed. Managing your symptoms of depression requires choosing the right combination of medication and therapy. If one treatment fails, talk to your healthcare provider. They can help you create a different treatment plan that may work better in helping you manage your condition.

Chapter 21:

How To Train Yourself to Be Optimistic and Positive

Positive thinking brings with it a whole host of benefits, such as better wellbeing and better sleep. To start reaping these benefits, check out how you can train your brain to be optimistic.

While many of us believe our happiness – or lack thereof – is based on external things, we're often the ones holding ourselves back. Many of us go through our days feeding ourselves negative messages we may not even be aware of, convincing ourselves we're "not good enough", "not clever enough" or "not attractive enough". To start thinking more positively, you need to change these messages. Try to look out for negative thoughts that pop into your head and replace them with positive messages. Write down some8 positive mantras and repeat them on a daily basis.

Most of us are happy to acknowledge other people's successes and accomplishments; however, when it comes to our own, we frequently play them down or ignore them entirely. To start thinking more positively about yourself, you need to regularly remind yourself of what you have – and can – achieve. Stop listening to your inner critic, reflect on your past achievements, and start to really appreciate your success and what you have to offer.

If you want to become an optimist, it can help to find yourself a positive role model. Whether it is a colleague, close friend or even a celebrity, think of the most unflappable, cheerful person you can. For the next few weeks, do an experiment and try to take a walk in their shoes. Whenever negativity starts creeping in or you find yourself in a difficult situation, think: "what would (insert name of chosen optimist) do?" Answer honestly, then try to follow suit.

It's important to remember that it isn't events themselves that make us unhappy, it is our interpretation and reaction to them, and while you can't always change events, you can change your response. When negative situations occur, try to reframe them by focusing on the positives or what you can learn from the situation. Maybe you have gained inner strength and resilience, grown closer to a friend through sharing your heartbreak or learned something about yourself. Try your best to focus on what you have learned and gained from your experience rather on than what you have lost. When things don't go right in life, optimists tend to view each incident as an isolated event, while pessimists often look out for patterns of bad luck and think "if it happened once, it'll happen again". However, it is important not to try to predict the future based on what has happened before. Remember that a plan or relationship failing doesn't make you a failure and just because something disappointing has happened once (or more) it doesn't mean it will happen again.

What is gone is gone, and how you deal with the aftermath is the most important thing. There is no point apportioning blame, either on yourself or others. You have the power to change a situation and move on. It is so easy to say 'I should have done things differently' with the benefit of hindsight. However, if bad things have happened, look at tomorrow as exactly what it is — a new day — in which good things can happen, if you let them.

Chapter 22:

How To Stop Judging Your Own Work

Have you been extra nice to yourself lately? If you're a writer ... the answer is probably: "...mayyyybe?"

Writers — creators in general — are way too hard on themselves. We like making things, and we feel good doing it. But we really want to feel like we're doing a good job.

When we don't feel that way — which happens much more often than we realize — we start to doubt if writing is even worth the struggle.

Why are we so judgmental of our own work? Because it's the easiest to judge. It comes from us. We know it better than anyone. But we can all learn to be critical without being so harsh. Here's how.

Remind yourself that not everything you write is going to feel polished.

And the simple reason for that? The majority of the time, it won't be.

You have to make messes to make masterpieces. You have to do things wrong, you have to not do your best if you're ever going to learn what you're actually capable of. If what you're writing seems terrible — well, it might be. That doesn't mean it always will be, or that it will be the best thing you'll ever write.

You're going to write sentences you're unsure of, paragraphs that just don't "sound quite right." You're going to question whether or not this scene should stay or go. You're going to ask yourself a million times if you're doing any of this right.

What matters most is that you keep writing anyway. You can't polish something unfinished. Even if a draft feels like the worst thing, you've ever written, at least you have something to work with — something you can improve little by little until it meets your personal standards (if that's even possible …).

Focus on how you feel about your work, not on how others might react.

We're all guilty of imagining how our future readers will react to certain parts of our stories. Sometimes, it's what keeps you going when you're

starting to feel unsure. When you laugh at your own writing (admit it —
it happens to you too), you picture others laughing too.

But there's a dark side to this train of thought. If we focus too much on
what people might think about our writing, we can begin to worry that
they won't like it. That they'll tell everyone else not to read it. That our
words aren't actually good … that they never will be.

The best way to judge whether or not your writing is meaningful and
readable is if it feels that way to you. Yes, your readers matter whether
they exist yet or not. You are writing for their entertainment. But until
you get your words in front of eyes, the only opinion that matters is yours.

Your inner critic will never stop talking, but you can tune it out.

Here's the truth not every writing expert will tell you: you will never stop
doubting or judging yourself or your writing. There is no magic cure for
self-criticism. But that doesn't mean you can't tone it down enough to
avoid letting it interfere with your work.

We judge ourselves more harshly than everyone else does (even though
it sometimes feels the other way around) because we genuinely want to
do a good job. And deep down we know we are the only ones in control
of whether or not we do the work "well."

The problem is, we're so used to seeing others' work and the kinds of writing that gets high praise that we often can't help but compare our drafts to their published masterpieces. When we do that, our writing just never feels "as good." We immediately spiral into "i'll never be good enough" self-talk. We get sad. We stop writing.

That negative self-talk will always be there. You will always hear it.But you don't have to listen to it. You don't have to care about the lies it's telling you. You don't have to let them stop you from doing the work you know you're meant to do.

It's one thing to say you're not going to pay attention to your voice of doubt and another to actually ignore it. It's not that simple for a lot of people — and that's ok. Some have an easier time quieting their minds than others. As a writer, it's often one of those things you learn to do the longer you do it, the more you practice it. That voice in your head telling you that you'll never achieve your dreams?

The best thing you can do to demote its scream to a whisper is to prove it wrong.

Chapter 23:

Happy People Choose to Exercise

There is a feeling you get when you just finish your workout, and you feel amazing, much better than you were feeling before. Even when you are not feeling motivated to go to the gym, just thinking about this feeling makes you get up, leave your bed and get going to the gym. This feeling can also be called an endorphin rush. Exercise indeed makes you happier in multiple ways.

Firstly, movement helps you bond with others that are in the brain chemistry of it all. Your heart rate is going up, you are using your body, engaging your muscles, your brain chemistry will change, and it will make it easier for you to connect and bond with other people. It also changes how your trust people. Research also showed that social pressures like a hug, laughing, or high-five are also enhanced. You will also find your new fitness fam, the people you will be working out with, and because you will have a shared interest that is having a healthy lifestyle will help you have a stronger bond with them. And as experts say that having strong relationships and connections in life will help you in overall happiness. We have already discussed those exercise increases endorphins but what you do not know is that it increases a lot more brain chemicals that make you feel happy and good about yourself. Some of the brain chemicals that increase are; dopamine, endorphins, endocannabinoid and adrenaline. All of these chemicals are associated with feeling confident, capable, and happy. The amount of stress, physical pain, and anxiety also decrease significantly. A chemical that your body creates when your muscles contract is called "myokine", it is also shown to boost happiness and relieve stress.

Secondly, exercise can help boost your confidence, and of course, when it comes to feeling empowered and happy, confidence is the key. "At the point when you move with others, it's anything but a solid feeling of 'greater than self' probability that causes individuals to feel more idealistic and enabled, "Also, it permits individuals to feel more engaged turning around the difficulties in their own lives. What's more, that is a fascinating side advantage of moving with others because there's an encapsulated feeling of 'we're in the same boat' that converts into self-assurance and the capacity to take on difficulties in your day; to day existence."

Thirdly, exercising outdoors affects your brain, similar to meditation. In case you're similar to the innumerable other people who have found out about the advantages of contemplation yet can't make the time, uplifting news. You may not need to contemplate to get a portion of the advantages. Researchers found that exercising outside can similarly affect the cerebrum and disposition as reflection. Exercising outside immediately affects a state of mind that is amazingly incredible for wretchedness and nervousness. Since it's anything but a state in your mind that is the same as contemplation, the condition of open mindfulness,"

Chapter 24:

How To Stop Being A Narcissist

Narcissists often get flak for being incapable of change.

The reason, according to psychologists, is that most narcissists aren't really aware of their narcissistic tendencies. These issues are often deep-seated, and self-preservation stops them from even recognizing their problems.

But chances are, if you're reading this, you're one of those who want to change. Admitting you might have Narcissistic Personality Disorder is already a step forward.

Self-aware narcissists can change. In this article, we've curated seven key steps on how to stop being a narcissist, according to some of the world's top psychology experts. We then go through the negative impacts of narcissism, followed by a discussion on whether narcissists can really change.

You have Narcissistic Personality Disorder if you:

- Think quite highly of yourself, like you're the only important person in the world.

- Are self-entitled and feel that you deserve nothing but the best.

- Demand recognition even if you didn't do anything to deserve it.

- Exaggerate your skills and achievements and brag about them excessively.
- Make everything about you.
- Use and manipulate people to get what you want.
- Unwilling to recognize and value the needs of others.

Overcoming narcissism is no simple process. Absolute change may be near impossible. However, you can make changes that will create a positive impact on your life.

Know What Your "Triggers" Are

Narcissistic behaviour often emerges when a person suffering from Narcissistic Personality Disorder gets "triggered."

According to Greenberg, "triggers" are: "…situations, words, or behaviours that arouse strong negative feelings in you. People with narcissistic issues tend to overreact when they are "triggered" and do things that they later regret."

As a first step, it's important to know in which situations your narcissism comes out. Learning what they are can help you identify the reasons behind your narcissism, so you may be able to handle them accordingly.

For example, if you experience narcissistic tendencies and want to become aware of your triggers, you may notice that you often feel a surge of anger when someone you perceive being of a "lower status" challenges your authority in the workplace

Or you may notice that you are often dismissive of other people when they suggest ideas.

Whatever your particular triggers are, start to take note of them. It may be useful to carry a notebook with you or jot them down in a note-taking app on your phone.

Over time, you'll start to notice patterns on when you feel triggered by others and react with narcissistic tendencies.

Manage Your Impulses

Narcissist people are often impulsive and make decisions without thinking of the consequences. If you display narcissist tendencies, it's important to emphasize thinking first and reacting later.

According to Greenberg: "Practice inhibiting or delaying your normal response when triggered. Your 'normal' response is the now unwanted one that you do automatically. It has become wired as a habit into the neurons of your brain."

The key step to changing your behaviours is to become aware of your impulses. This gives you the opportunity to create behavioural change in your life.

Taking note of your triggers as recommended in step one will teach you to create some space between the stimulus of the trigger and your response. Pausing when triggered opens up the opportunity to create a new set of behaviours

Chapter 25:

Focus - The Art of Alignment

Focus. A buzzword in the workspace. Everyone wants to have focus and keep focus. If you want it, you got to understand it. Focus is not some abstract notion that comes and goes as it pleases. It only seems like that because you haven't learnt the rhythm of focus. Do you know what lures it in? Do you know what keeps it there once it comes?

Because at its core, focus is quite simple. If we look at a laser, we see a focussed beam of light, how? Lasers are concentrated light waves, in order for it to work the waves have to be coming from the same base, be going in the same direction, and be almost perfectly in sync.

Let me tell you that if you need to know who you are and what you want, because otherwise nothing will be coming from the same base. Everything that you do should stem from knowing who you are and who you want to be. If you know those two things then you start to bring everything into that bigger picture, you start every activity from that foundation.

If you want to be a professional athlete, then you go to your office job knowing that this is just a means to support your training and future career. You know that the better you perform there the closer you become to financial freedom and the more you can invest time into the thing you want to become. Not only will that motivate you to push through the mundane, but you will find constant fulfilment because everything you do will seem to bring you closer to your goals. Even if they are not related at all. If you are looking to become the CEO of a big company, then you take the time to focus on cleaning your house because you cannot expect to bring order outside of your home if you do not have control within it.

Your first step to focus is finding your base and your direction, knowing who you are and who you want to be. Then you bring everything in sync with that. Because when everything flows in the patterns of your passion, focus is inevitable.

What about a camera? They focus by shifting the lens towards and away from the film. This means the light converges before or directly on the film, or it doesn't get to converge at all. When light converges all the points of it line up in a way that produces a clear picture. The art of photography is finding positioning it in such a way that what you want to capture is focussed. If you want to capture first place, if you want to get that promotion, whatever you want to do. You need to be able to adjust your focus so that the things you want are clear, and everything else blurs slightly into the background. Blurring does not distort your vision, it brings clarity to the primary focus. It ensures the desirable image of the future is sharp which means allowing the obstacles to blur into the process. When your focus is right, you don't get tempted by distractions. You see the bigger picture in light of your goals, not the deviations from them.

Chapter 26:

Ten Habits Of The Rich And Successful

The rich and successful have common habits. Some of them have walked down the same path to glory.

Wealth is not measured in terms of properties only but also the strength of character. One can be rich in wisdom but not as much in properties. Nevertheless, they are considered rich and successful because they have an abundance of an intangible asset – wisdom.

Here are ten habits of the rich and successful:

1. They Are Generous

Rich and successful people are often generous because they know what it feels like to lack. Even those born in rich families are generous because they probably have seen their parents helping the needy.

Most rich people globally have foundations in their name. It is not a channel to wealth for themselves, but a means to do acts of charity. The Bill & Melinda gates foundation, for example, has helped the most vulnerable globally during a famine, war, and even during the coronavirus disease pandemic.

2. They Read Widely

Successful people read a lot. The reading culture in them developed at an early age and could have most likely molded them into the people they are. Great leaders are readers. As leaders of giant corporates, it is important to be well vast with the wisdom of other great people.

Reading is not capped at any age. Successful people know that learning is continuous and apply the knowledge from the literature they read in their lives. Reading lightens the burden of management on the shoulders of the rich who are directors in their companies.

3. They Are Not Workaholics

It is amazing how one can be wealthy and successful without being a workaholic. Ironically, most workaholics are not as rich as you would expect. Despite them foregoing a lot of things for the sake of their work, they cannot match the rich who work only a few hours a day.

It is not the amount of time you work but the quality of work you do. Work holism will rob you of your social life and you will be depressed. Apportion equal time in everything you do, not only your work.

4. They Are Social People

One would think that most rich and successful people are arrogant or anti-social. This is untrue. They are social and outgoing. You will find them in their social circles over coffee or playing golf. They are approachable and receptive to new ideas.

Reaching them is indeed difficult because of their security or protocol to follow before talking to them. They have security because of their high profile, and they could be targets of bad people. Nevertheless, they are very engaging when you get to know them.

5. They Have Trust Issues

Most rich people are insecure because of their wealth. They rarely trust strangers because their intentions are unknown. Some of them have been short-changed in their business dealings and cannot easily trust again.

When interacting with them, do not take offense to their mistrust. Instead, try to win their trust slowly until they realize that you are genuine. It is only then that they will trust you with their work or build a friendship with you.

6. They Are Never Idle

An idle mind is the devil's workshop. The rich and successful know this too well. You may be tempted into doing immoral acts when you have a lot of idle time at your disposal. Engage yourself willfully in productive activities lest you are lured into vices because you have a lot of free time. This is not a call to work holism. It is okay to have free time to spend out of your busy schedule, but that time should be planned for carefully. Like the rich and successful, your mind should always be occupied with positive thoughts and plans on how you can progress.

7. They Have A Flexible Mindset

The rich and successful do not lead rigid lives. They have a flexible mindset that makes them open to other business ideas and suggestions. Their ears listen to consumer needs in the market and they develop products and services to meet those needs.

It is often misconceived that successful people live in their zone and are indifferent to common people. The truth is that they became successful by being open-minded. A fixed mind is an enemy of progress.

8. They Are Bold

Wealthy people are bold and make public statements without any fear of backlash. Boldness is a sign of being an alpha.

As much as their wealth could be insulation against any repercussions, people pay attention when the rich give their opinions because they are unsure of their motive. When a successful person boldly gives their opinion, it is taken seriously because it has the potential to influence market forces.

9. They Consult Widely

The rich are not always wise; even the wise seek counsel. Before they make any significant action, they seek advice from people they trust. They then weigh the pros and cons of what they intended to do and make an informed choice.

Unlike common people who act out of impulse, the rich take advice from trusted sources (mostly professionals) very seriously. Rarely do they err, always hitting the nail on the head. You should consider consulting before acting if you want to be like the rich.

10. They Are Visionary

Vision is often misconstrued for sight. It is getting the bigger picture without losing grip on fine details. Were it not for the eagle vision of the successful, they could not be able to maintain their status. Rich people know the direction they are going, and they work towards it.

Vision is not an innate trait; it is developed over time. You will need to be visionary and not get distracted as you chart your way towards richness. Take this cue from successful people.

In conclusion, we acknowledge that the rich and successful run the world. When you start practicing their habits, you will soon be like them.

Chapter 27:

6 Ways To Adopt A Better Lifestyle For Long-Term Success

A good lifestyle leads to a good life. The important choices we make throughout our lives impact our future in numerous ways. The need to make ourselves better in every aspect of life and the primary ability to perform such a routine can be a lifestyle. There is no proper way to live written in a book; however, through our shared knowledge and our comprehension, we can shape a lifestyle that can be beneficial and exciting at the same time. Though there is no doubt that falling into a specific routine can be difficult but, maintaining a proper state is more critical for a successful life.

For long-term success, a good lifestyle is a priority. Almost everything we do in our lives directly or indirectly involves our future self. So, a man needs to become habitual of such things that can profit him in every way possible. To visualize a better you, you need to configure just about everything around you. And to change all the habits that may make you feel lagging.

The most common feature of a better lifestyle for long-term success is determination.

1. Change in Pattern Of Your Life

It is good to shape a pattern of living from the start and forming good habits, engaging yourself in profitable practice, and choosing a healthier custom. It feels impossible to change something you have already been habitual of, but willpower is the key. With some motivation and dedication, you can change yourself into a better version of yourself. You are choosing what might be suitable for you and staying determined on that thought. The first step is to let go of harmful things slowly because letting go of habits and patterns that you are used to can be challenging. After some, sometimes you will notice yourself letting go of things more easily.

2. Take Your Time

Time is an essential factor when it comes to forming a lifestyle for a successful life. Time can seem to slow through the process, making us think that it may have been stopped in our most difficult moments. Similarly, making us feel it goes flying by when our life is relaxed and at ease. Time never stops for anyone. It is crucial to make sure we make most of our time and consume it in gaining more knowledge and power.

Take time to inform your lifestyle, but not more than required. We are taking things at a moderate pace so you can both enjoy life and do work.

3. Don't Always Expect Things to Go Your Way

As much as we humans like to get our hopes high, we can't always expect things to go our way. Even things we have worked hard for can sometimes go downhill. It is at times overconfidence, but sometimes it can be pure bad luck. We can't get disheartened by something that was not meant to go a specific way. Don't expect perfection in all the work you do. Staying patient is the walk towards the reward. And making the best out of the worst can be the only way to get yourself going.

4. Don't Be Afraid to Ask For Help

It is human nature to ask each other for help now and then. If it comes to this point, don't be afraid to ask for help yourself. Ask someone superior to aid you on matters you find difficult. Don't hesitate to ask your inferiors who might have more knowledge than you in some certain customs. Help them, too, if needed. Ask them to assist you out on points, but never make them do the whole project. Don't make someone do something you wouldn't do yourself.

5. Be Prompt In Everything

Lagging behind your work can be the worst possible habit you could raise. Make yourself punctual in every aspect. Make sure you are on time everywhere. Either it's to wake up in the morning or to go to a meeting. Laziness can never be proven good for you or your dream towards a prosperous lifestyle. Respect time, and it shall respect you. Show your colleges that they can depend on you to show up on time and take responsibility for work. You would rather wait than making others wait for you. That will show you seriousness toward your business.

6. Keep A Positive Attitude

Keeping a positive attitude can lead to a positive lifestyle. Be happy with yourself in every context, and make sure that everything you do has your complete confidence. Be thankful to all who surround you. Keep a positive attitude, whether it be a home or office. Speak with your superiors with respect and make yourself approachable around inferiors. Your positive mindset can affect others in a way too. They will become more inclined towards you, and they can easily suggest you help someone.

Conclusion

Just about everything in your life affects your future in a way or other, so make sure that you do all you can to make yourself worth the praise. Keep your lifestyle simple but effective. Try to do as much as possible for yourself and make time to relax as well. For long-term success, willpower is the most important; make sure you have it. Keep your headlight and calm for the upcoming difficulties and prepare yourself to face almost everything life throws at you.

Chapter 28:

6 Ways To Adopt New Actions That Will Be Beneficial To Your Life

There is this myth that goes around saying that, once you leave your teenage, you can never change your Habits. One can analyze this for themselves. Everyone has a list of new year's resolutions and goals. We hope to get these things done to some extent, but never do we ever really have a clear idea of how to get to those goals in the least possible time.

We always desire a better future but never really know how to bring the necessary change in our lives. The change we need is a change in attitude and behavior towards life altogether. Change is never easy, but it is achievable with some sheer willpower. You might be on the right track to lead a better life, but there are always more and better things to add to your daily habits that can be helpful in your daily life.

Here are 6 simple yet achievable actions you need to take:

1. Decide Today What Is Most Important In Your Life

Life is a constant search for motivation. The motivation to keep doing and changing for the better. Once you have something to change for, take a moment and envision the rest of your life with and without the change you are about to make.

If you have made up your mind, now think about how you can start off with these things. For starters, if you want a healthy lifestyle, start your day with a healthy breakfast and morning exercise on an empty stomach. If you want to scale your business, make a customer-friendly business model.

2. Make Reasonable and Achievable Goals

Adopting new habits can be challenging, especially if you have to change something in your day-to-day life to get better results. Start easy by making goals that are small, easy, reasonable, and won't give you a headache.

You can start off with baby steps. If you want to become more responsible, mature, and sorted in your life, just start your day by making your own bed, and do your dishes. Ride a bicycle to work, instead of a car or a bus. Things become smooth and easier once you have a reason for the hard acts.

3. Erase Distractions from Your Daily Life

You have wasted a lot already, don't waste any more time. As young as you are right now, you should feel more privileged than the older people around you. You have got the luxury of time over them. You have the right energy and pinnacle moments to seize every opportunity you can grasp.

Don't make your life a cluster of meaningless and profit-less distractions. You don't have to go to every public gathering that you are invited to. Only those that give you something in return. Something that you can avail yourself of in your years to come. Don't divulge in these distractions only for the sake of memories. Memories fade but the time you waste will always have its imprint in every moment that follows.

4. Make a Diary and a Music Playlist

You can devote some time to yourself, just to communicate with your brain and start a discussion with yourself. Most people keep a diary for this purpose, some people tend to make a digital one these days. When you start writing to yourself in the third person, talking and discussing your issues and your weaknesses, you tend to find the solutions within.

Most people find it comforting and calming when they have a playlist of music playing in the background while working. Everyone can try this to check if they get a better level of creativity if they have some small activity that soothes their stressed nerves.

5. Incorporate Regular Walk and Exercise in Your Life

When you know you have a whole day ahead of you, where you have to sit in an office chair for the next 8 hours. Where you have to sit in your home office looking at those sheets for most of the day. A 10 min walk before or after the busy schedule can help a lot in such conditions. You can never avoid physical activities for your whole life, especially if you want to live a healthier and longer life.

People always feel reluctant to exercise and running once they enter college or work life. Especially once they have a family to look out for. But trust me, your body needs that blood rushing once a day for some time. You will feel much more pumped and motivated after a hard 2-mile jog or a 15 min workout.

6. Ask Others for Help and Advice

You have a life to live for yourself, but always remember, you are never too old to ask for help. A human can never perfect something in their life. You will always find someone better than you at a particular task, don't shy to ask for help, and never hold back to ask for any advice.

We feel low many a time in our lives. Sometimes we get some foul thoughts, but we shouldn't ever pounce on them. We should rather seek someone's company for comfort and sharing our concerns.

Conclusion

The ultimate success in life is the comfort you get at the end of every day. Life can never be fruitful, beneficial, and worth living for if we don't arrange our lives as resourceful human beings. Productive minds always find a way to counter things and make the best out of everything, and this is the art of living your life.

Chapter 29:

Excuses – the Maxed Out

Pity-Card

SHUT UP!

I don't want to hear it.

I'm not here to empathise with you. That's not my role. I'm here to call you out. You have been playing the pity card for far too long and now you've maxed out your credit. It's being declined. No more woe-is-me cheques to cover for your inadequacies. No more feeling sorry for yourself. Apologies are supposed to be a commitment to change. Uh oh. That means you gotta get up off your couch and do something.

Nobody is going to come to your pity party so take of your dunce-cap party hat and start cleaning up your act. Because excuses aren't going to cut it anymore. It doesn't matter why you think you can't do something because the fact of the matter is that your probably can. If single moms can work three jobs and run a household of four kids, you can make the time to go to gym. If children in Africa can walk several kilometres just to go to school, then I'm pretty confident you can make the time for that project you're supposed to be working on.

The fact of the matter is that it is not about time or energy or even money. If you wanted it badly enough you could come up with more than enough of any one of those things. Heck, if you just put as much time into you dreams as you do into making excuses for why you're not achieving them you might already have!

The things you tell yourself, the things you complain about to your spouse or your colleagues – they are not holding you back! YOU ARE! You have the vision, you have the passion, you have the potential and you DO HAVE THE CAPACITY. The only thing you don't have is the right narrator. You have some whiny toddler in your head who refuses to believe that you can. But that stubbornness in failure can be converted to assuredness of success. You just need to change the narrative. Change the storyline. Every time you catch yourself making an excuse come up with a reason why you can do it. Or drop whatever you are doing and take 5 minutes to work on it right then and there.

The only way to pay off your excuse's debt is by working on the things you said you could never do. You owe the greatness bank a whole lot of potential and you can only pay it back by TAKING ACTION. Go to they gym and pay some off it off, hone your skill and pay some of it off. Register your company, buy the URL and get the patent and soon you will find yourself earning interest. You will start making money from them instead of paying it back.

The moment you realise your capacity is the moment you increase your capital. So shut your mouth, open your eyes, and apply yourself. Because excuses are a debt you can no longer afford.

Chapter 30:

How To Deal With Loss (Business And Career)

Whether you've witnessed layoffs, early retirement, or contract termination, job loss is one of life's most stressful events. In addition to the apparent financial pain it can cause, job loss stress can also seriously affect your mood, relationships, and overall mental and emotional health.

Our work is often more than just a way to make money. They affect how we see ourselves and how others see us. Even if you don't like your job, it will exit from society and give your life structure, purpose and meaning. Quitting a job suddenly can make you resentful, angry, or depressed. They may doubt their identity, grieve over everything they have lost, or worry about the future.

Depending on your job loss situation, you may feel like your employer has been betrayed, you may not have the power to lead your life, or you may blame yourself for any flaws or mistakes. Stress and anxiety can be overwhelming. But while things look grim right now, there is hope. With time and appropriate coping skills, you can overcome these obstacles, relieve stress and anxiety, and continue working.

Losing your job can make each day feel terrible but find something to be grateful for. It can be anything, even if you feel thankful for your bed now. Many studies show that gratitude can dramatically improve mental health and well-being. It can help us rethink our worldview, preventing us from becoming depressed or motivated. It can remind us that we have a lot to be thankful for things we didn't think of and that everything will be fine. Try to keep a gratitude journal where you physically record one thing you are grateful for each day. Set a time, for example, right after waking up or before bedtime. Or, if you have other daily routines, reinforce them. This is called 'habit accumulation' and should not be forgotten.

Now that you've got an idea of how to deal with the most overwhelming emotions and try to rethink with gratitude let's look at some ways to deal with job loss in different areas of your life.

An emergency fund is the best buffer against surprises like unexpected job loss. This will ensure you and your family have enough money to cover the roof, cover utilities, and pay for daily necessities. Think of it as life insurance.

Join an association, find a few freelance jobs, participate in online business events, and find exam consulting jobs. If your employer asks, "What did you do while you were out of work?" There is no reason to worry.

Keeping up with new trends and preferred companies will give you the confidence to start a conversation and help you identify new opportunities. Even if you have multiple blanks on your resume, working knowledge in the industry will make you a potential candidate. How can you keep up with new trends? Reading blogs and other publications relevant to your industry is your best bet.

Modern businesses review their social media profiles before inviting them for an interview, making sure everything is orderly and welcoming. Also, try to be consistent with what you say on your profile (at least make sure your job is mentioned the same way on LinkedIn, Twitter, and others).

Expand your resources and keep an open mind when looking for opportunities. Explore social media, recruitment pages, job sites, local newspapers and business sites. You never know which channel or platform will be the source of a new job.

This cannot be avoided. Unemployment is a challenging experience. But I believe there are too many opportunities to get out of this for a better place than you started. Perhaps you will have a chance to find a job or start a business. It will better suit your skills and hobbies, or you will have new personal or professional connections you could never have made otherwise. No matter where this road takes you, try to keep your head up and your eyes looking straight ahead. Find the positives and opportunities in everything you're experiencing and use them as opportunities to explore ideas and improve what you thought you didn't have the time or flexibility to do. You can handle it.

Chapter 31:

How To Spend Money Wisely?

Financial struggles could be of many types, I.E., Not bringing in enough money, not spending money wisely, or simply spending more money than making. According to time, nearly 73% of Americans die in debt. Sure, we're guilty of slipping up at one point or the other. It's quite easy to fall into the habit of buying expensive coffee every day, eating out or ordering takeaways, and getting our hands on groceries that we have eventually ended up throwing out. We don't have to be an expert in personal finances nor have A big investment portfolio to be financially secure. It is, however, essential to understand the basics of financial planning.

Before you can start figuring out how to spend your money wisely, you need to analyse and understand where exactly your money is going. Make A budget to track both your expenses and your income. Once you get your hands on where the money is going, you can start looking for better opportunities where they could be spent instead.

Need I tell you that far too many purchases are impulse decisions? It can be fine on A shorter scale, like buying A $1 chocolate, but it can become A serious problem for larger purchases. Before you buy something, think about A few factors first; like how it's going to affect you in the future, how long is it going to last, is it going to put you in debt, is the value you will get out of it over its lifetime worth the cost. These are the questions that you really should ask yourself to determine if the product is worth buying or are you only satisfying your inner cravings.

The average person spends far too much money in trying to maintain an image in front of others. Fancy cars, brand-name clothing, expensive watches, and perfumes, all these that we buy have more to do with impressing others than it does with purchasing something that we want to enjoy. This pursuit is far too expensive and unnecessary. Buy the things that you enjoy yourself and never fall prey to the feeling that you have to spend your money in bulk to impress people.

After you have started to track your finances, you can keep an eye on the habits that may be draining your budget. These habits could include expensive hobbies, eating out too much, stress shopping, spending loads of money on your friends/partner, or any number of other financial drains. Once you have figured out which habits are eating up large portions of your income, you can then self-evaluate whether these habits are actually worth your money or not.

Some people are naturally good at saving money. They draw enjoyment from growing their wealth. While for others, money is something that is spent the moment it reaches their hands. Anything else feels like A wasted opportunity for them. If you find yourself falling in the latter category, try and adopt A mentality that values savings over products. In the end, money spent on products that will wear or become uninteresting will always be lesser than money invested, or money saved that will always benefit you.

Spending your money wisely isn't always about just avoiding unnecessary purchases - it also requires you to take the money that you save and put it towards your financial goals. With that in mind, it's never going to be about starting investing too early or too late. No matter how young or old you are, invest your money in things that will benefit you. Your spent money growing in value as time goes on is always A wise use of it.

Chapter 32:

How To Accept Yourself No Matter What

There are many reasons why it may be difficult to accept yourself. Just hearing one that resonates for you can bring relief because you realize you are not alone — someone else has been there, someone else understands. Here are some of the reasons self-acceptance can be hard and the antidotes you can practice to gradually accept yourself more and more— step one and two from the change steps listed above.

See which ones resonate for you.

1. You Think You're at Fault

You may blame yourself for something that happened in your life, especially events that may have occurred in your early years. For example, you may believe you're the cause of conflict in your parents' relationship or even their divorce.

Antidote: give the responsibility back. It was never yours to own.

2. You Think You're Not Worthy

You began to feel inadequate as a child and carried that belief into your adult life.

Antidote: you are worthy simply because you exist. In between your confusion, self-doubt, and angst, there is so much goodness in you. Instead of focusing on your failings, start to believe in and accentuate your positives. Take time to learn to love yourself

3. You Didn't Have Positive Roles Models

If one of your parents or primary caregivers didn't accept themselves, you may be modelling their behavior.

Antidote: find positive roles models now, people who love, accept and care for themselves with confidence. Follow their lead.

4. You've Made Self-Acceptance Conditional

You believe you need to achieve something before you can fully accept yourself. You're waiting to complete your education, earn a specific amount of money, or get a promotion at your job.

But even when you make it to a goal post, you find you still can't accept yourself. You tell yourself you need to reach the next before you do.

Antidote: take the conditions off and accept your whole self right, now.

5. You Are Trying To Live Up To Societal Norms

There's so much pressure to live up to societal norms within most families, at school, and in the advertisements that abound all around you.

You may not accept who you are because you think you should be someone else—the grade a student or the perfect mom and wife with the ideal figure and a corporate job too.

Antidote: break the societal norms! Make new ones! Make your own! Decide who you want to be for yourself.

6. Your Circle Is Not Supportive

It's difficult to feel good about yourself if your partner, friends, or employer are constantly putting you down. I know this for myself. I had a harsh boss for many years. His constant criticism eroded my self-confidence.

Antidote: surround yourself with people who love, appreciate, and support you, one person at a time. Leave unsupportive situations.

7. You've Been Traumatized

The experience of shock or early childhood trauma can trigger shame or the mistaken belief that you were somehow responsible.

Antidote: know this is a common reaction in trauma, but it doesn't make it true. Find a trauma therapist who can help you heal the trauma and transform these incorrect beliefs.

You can't go from zero self-acceptance to accepting yourself just like that. But it doesn't have to take eons either.

Positive repetition works over time. It actually modifies your brain. Use these four steps to change your response:

1. "first, label the response you want to change."

2. "second, identify the new response that you want to develop."

3. "third, explore what factors might reduce the unwanted response and boost the desired response."

4. "lastly, repeatedly practice the new response so that it becomes ingrained."

Start on the path of self-acceptance now. You'll feel very different in a few months and surely in a few years to come. You'll grow in self-love, self-acceptance, and your ability to care for yourself.

Won't that be so much better than rejecting yourself?

Chapter 33:

Happy People Use Their Character Strengths

One of the most popular exercises in the science of positive psychology (some argue it is the single most popular exercise) is referred to as "use your signature strengths in new ways." But what does this exercise mean? How do you make the most of it to benefit yourself and others?

On the surface, the exercise is self-explanatory:

a. Select one of your highest strengths – one of your character strengths that is core to who you are, is easy for you to use, and gives you energy;

b. Consider a new way to express the strength each day;

c. Express the strength in a new way each day for at least 1 week.

Studies repeatedly show that this exercise is connected with long-term benefits (e.g., 6 months) such as higher levels of happiness and lower levels of depression.

Put The Exercise Into Practice

In practice, however, people sometimes find it surprisingly challenging to come up with new ways to use one of their signature strengths. This is because we are very accustomed to using our strengths. We frequently use our strengths mindlessly without much awareness. For example, have you paid much attention to your use of self-regulation as you brush your teeth? Your level of prudence or kindness while driving? Your humility while at a team meeting?

For some strengths, it is easy to come up with examples. Want to apply curiosity in a new way? Below is a sample mapping of what you might do. Keep it simple. Make it complex. It's up to you!

- On Monday, take a new route home from work and explore your environment as you drive.
- On Tuesday, ask one of your co-workers a question you have not previously asked them.
- On Wednesday, try a new food for lunch – something that piques your curiosity to taste.
- On Thursday, call a family member and explore their feelings about a recent positive experience they had.
- On Friday, take the stairs instead of the elevator and explore the environment as you do.
- On Saturday, as you do one household chore (e.g., washing the dishes, vacuuming), pay attention to 3 novel features of the activity while you do it. Example: Notice the whirring sound of

the vacuum, the accumulation of dust swirling around in the container, the warmth of the water as you wash the dishes, the sensation of the weight of a single plate or cup, and so on.

- On Sunday, ask yourself 2 questions you want to explore about yourself – reflect or journal your immediate responses.
- Next Monday….keep going!

Widening The Scope

In some instances, you might feel challenged to come up with examples. Let me help. After you choose one of your signature strengths, consider the following 10 areas to help jolt new ideas within you and stretch your approach to the strength.

How might I express the character strength…

- At work
- In my closest relationship
- While I engage in a hobby
- When with my friends
- When with my parents or children
- When I am alone at home
- When I am on a team
- As the leader of a project or group
- While I am driving
- While I am eating

Chapter 34:

Happy People Find Reasons to Laugh and Forge Deep Connections

"…Making a connection with men and women through humour, happiness and laughter not only helps you make new friends, but it is the means to establish a strong, meaningful connection to people."

People always try to have a personality that attracts people and makes them feel comfortable around them. Utilizing their humour has been one of those ways to create new friendships. But once you start doing this, you will realize that this humorous nature has emotions and attitudes that comprise happiness and positivity. This will also help you create deep and meaningful connections that will last a lifetime.

When you intend to focus on humour to find deep connections, your subconscious mind starts focusing on positivity. You will slowly turn out to be more positive in your reasoning and conduct because awareness of what's funny is truly only demonstrative of one's very own bliss. In this manner, you're sustaining a more appealing, and that's just the beginning "contagious" attitude. Similarly, as we search out bliss in our everyday lives through satisfying work, leisure activities, individual interests and day to day life, so too do people seek out and wish to be encircled by joy on a relational level: joy and bitterness are contagious, and we as a whole wish to get the happy bug.

Humour helps fashion friendships since we wish to encircle ourselves with individuals who are glad. This way, our objective shouldn't just be to utilize humour to make new companions, however to zero in on the entirety of the uplifting perspectives and feelings that include an entertaining and carefree nature. By embodying satisfaction, inspiration, happiness, receptiveness, and tranquillity, we sustain a more grounded and "contagious" state of being.

Historically there was a negative connotation attached to humor, but over the years, research was done, and it proved otherwise. In any case, research on humor has come into the daylight, with humor currently seen as a character strength. Good brain science, a field that analyzes what individuals progress admirably, notes that humor can be utilized to cause others to feel better, acquire closeness, or help buffer pressure. Alongside appreciation, expectation and otherworldliness, a funny bone has a place with the arrangement of qualities positive clinicians call greatness; together, they help us manufacture associations with the world and give significance to life. Enthusiasm for humor corresponds with different qualities, as well, like insight and love of learning. Furthermore, humor exercises or activities bring about expanded sensations of passionate prosperity and idealism.

Once you step into adulthood, it can be difficult for many people to form friendships and then keep up with them because all of us get busier in our lives. Still, it's never too much to go to a bar and strike up a conversation with a random person and believe us, if you have a good sense of humor, they will be naturally attracted towards you.

Chapter 35:

Happy People Spend Time Alone

No man is an island except for similarly as we blossom with human contact and connections, so too would we be able to prosper from time burned through alone. Also, this, maybe, turns out to be particularly important right now since we're all in detachment. We've since quite a while ago slandered the individuals who decide to be distant from everyone else, except isolation shouldn't be mistaken for forlornness. Here are two mental reasons why investing energy in isolation makes us more joyful and more satisfied:

1. Spending Time Alone Reconnects Us

Our inclination for isolation might be transformative, as indicated by an examination distributed in the British Journal of Psychology in 2016. Utilizing what they call "the Savannah hypothesis of satisfaction," transformative clinicians Satoshi Kanazawa of the London School of Economics and Norman Li of Singapore Management University accept that the single, tracker accumulate way of life of our precursors structure the establishment of what satisfies us in present-day times. The group examined a study of 15,000 individuals matured somewhere between 18 and 28 in the United States. They found that individuals living in more thickly populated regions were fundamentally less cheerful than the individuals who lived in more modest networks.

"The higher the populace thickness of the prompt climate, the less glad" respondents were. The scientists accept this is because we had advanced mentally from when mankind, for the most part, existed on distant, open savannahs. Since quite a while ago, we have instilled an inclination to be content alone, albeit current life generally neutralizes that. Also, as good to beat all, they tracked down that the more clever an individual was, the more they appreciated investing energy alone. Along these lines, isolation makes you more joyful AND is evidence of your smarts. We're in.

2. Spending Time Alone Teaches Us Empathy

Investing in a specific measure of energy alone can create more compassion towards others than a milestone concentrate from Harvard. Scientists found that when enormous gatherings of individuals encircle us, it's harder for us to acquire viewpoints and tune into the sensations of others. However, when we venture outside that unique circumstance, the extra headspace implies we can feel for the situation of individuals around us in a more genuine and significant manner. Furthermore, that is uplifting news for others, but different investigations show that compassion and helping other people are significant to prosperity and individual satisfaction.

"At the point when you invest energy with a specific friend network or your colleagues, you foster a 'we versus them' attitude," clarifies psychotherapist and creator Amy Morin. "Investing energy alone assists you with growing more empathy for individuals who may not find a way into your 'inward circle.' "On the off chance that you're not used to isolation, it can feel awkward from the outset," she adds. "However, making that tranquil time for yourself could be critical to turning into the best form of yourself."

Chapter 36:

Happy People Plan Their Week in Advance for Maximum Productivity

There you are, enjoying a perfectly beautiful Sunday evening. You've had an eventful and fun weekend and decided to spend tonight chillaxing. Then, from out of nowhere, a sense of dread washes over you (there arose such a clatter?). Your mind begins to think about what you need to get done this week. There's just no way to stop these thoughts once they get rolling.

But how exactly should you plan your week so that it will be more productive? Well, here are two tips that will guarantee that your week will be efficient and effective.

1. Get a Head Start

"Sunday clears away the rust of the whole week." — Joseph Addison

It's true. If you want to have a productive week, then you need to start planning on Sundays. If that's not your cup of tea, though, then at least begin your preparations on Friday afternoon or Saturday.

I know. You want to kick back and relax this weekend. But, is it going to be the end of the world if you do a little work? Could you map out your week while watching football or waiting for your favorite HBO to start?

Set aside about an hour and jot down everything you need to get done this week. In particular, think about your daily routines, recurring events, deadlines, and goals. Next, mark them off first so that nothing else gets scheduled ahead of them. Don't forget about anything else that you've penciled in. Remember you are going to that concert with a friend or your family coming to town?

That may sound like a lot of work. But it gets all of these commitments out of your head. From there, you can begin to plan accordingly. For example, because you have family arriving on Thursday, you'll probably want to make sure that you get your most important work done in advance so that you can spend time with them.

2. Use The E/N/D System

The E/N/D system, which stands for Energizing / Neutral / Draining, can be used to help you prioritize your time. It accomplishes this by helping you manage your energy.

Whenever scheduling tasks, designate them as either E, N, or D. Usually, energizing tasks are the things you enjoy doing. As such, you would want to schedule them when you need an energy boost, like after lunch. Draining tasks are those that you dread because they're challenging. Those should be scheduled when you have the most energy, like in the morning.

Chapter 37:

Fight Lethargy and Win

Life is a continuous grind. Life is the summation of our efforts. Life is series of things that no one thinks can happen. But they do, and they do for a reason. Your life is no different than anyone else. You have the same needs and somewhat the same goals. But you might still be a failure while the world moves on. Let me explain why.

People always misunderstand having a humble mindset as opposed to having a go-getter mindset. The difference between you and a successful person is the difference in mindset.

When you think that you are not feeling well today to go to the gym. That you are not motivated enough to do some cardio or run that treadmill. That you didn't have a good day and now you are feeling down so you should stay in bed because you think you deserve some time off. This is the moment you messed up your life.

What you should have done is to tell yourself, what have I achieved today that made me deserving of this time off. You didn't!

How can you sit back and remain depressed when no one else feels sorry for you but only you do? Because you still haven't come to realize that no one will give you sympathy for something you made a mess of. And you are still not willing enough to make things happen for yourself.

When you have nothing, you think someone owes you something. That someone handles something bad that happens in your life. The reality is far from this.

It is fine if you are going through some rough patch in your life right now. But don't try to put the blame on others and back off of your responsibilities and duties. You have something to move towards but you are still sitting there waiting for the moment to come to your doorstep. But it ain't gonna happen. It's never an option to wait!

Don't just sit there and make strategies and set goals. Get up and start acting on those plans. The next plan will come by default.

You shouldn't feel depressed about the bad things, you should feel anger for why did you let those things happen to you in the first place. What did you lag that made you come to this stage right now. Why were you so lazy enough to let those results slide by you when your gut told you to do something different. But you didn't. And now it has all come to haunt you once again.

But you don't need that attitude. What you need is to stop analyzing and start doing something different rather than contemplate what you could have done.

The moments you lost will never come back, so there is no point in feeling sorry for those moments in this present moment. Use this moment to get the momentum you need.

Now is the time to prove yourself wrong, to make this life worth living for.

Now is the time to spend the most valuable asset of your life on something you want the most in your life. Now is the time to use all that energy and bring a change to your life that you will cherish for the rest of your life and in that afterlife.

Prove to yourself that you are worthy of that better life. That no one else deserves more than you. Because you made a cause for yourself. You ran all your life and struggled for that greater good.

Destiny carves its path when your show destiny what you have to offer.

You want to succeed in life, let me tell you the simplest way to that success; get up, go outside and get to work.

When you feel the lowest in your life, remember, you only start to lose that fat, when you start to sweat, and you feel the heat and the pain coming through.

What you started yesterday, finish it today. Not tomorrow, not tonight, but right now!

Get working! It doesn't matter if it takes you an hour or 12 to complete the job. Do it. You will never fulfill the task if you keep thinking for the right moment. Every moment is the right moment.

You are always one decision away from a completely different life. You are always one moment away from the best moment of your life. But it is either this moment or it's never.

Chapter 38:

8 Ways to Discover What's Holding You Back From Achieving Your Visions

We all have dreams, and I have no questions; you have made attempts at seeking after your goals. Oh, as a general rule, life's battles get the better of you and keep you down. The pressure of everyday life, again and again, puts you down. Regardless of your determination, devotion, and want, alone, they are not enough.

Being here exhibits you are not able to settle for a mediocre life and hidden desires. To help you in your goal of seeking after your objectives, you must become acquainted with those things keeping you down. When you do, you will want to eliminate every single reason keeping you down.

1. Fear

The deep-rooted foe is very likely a critical factor in keeping many of you from seeking after your objectives. It prevents you from acting, making you scared of venturing out. Dread is the thing that keeps you down. Dread is one reason why we don't follow what we truly need throughout everyday life.

• Fear of disappointment
• Fear of dismissal
• Fear of mocking
• Fear of disappointment

Quit allowing your feelings of fear to keep you down!

2. Procrastination

Putting things off till the following week, one month from now, one year from now, and regularly forever. You're not exactly sure the thing you're hanging tight for, but rather when whatever it happens, you'll be prepared to start seeking after your objectives. Be that as it may, this day never comes. Your fantasy stays as just a fantasy. Putting things off can just keep you down.

Quit allowing your Procrastination to keep you down!

3. Justifications

Do you find yourself procrastinating and making excuses for why you can't start working toward your goals? Those that succeed in accomplishing their objectives can overcome obstacles. So many individuals make excuses for themselves, believing they can't achieve a better career, start their own business, or find their ideal lifemate.

• It isn't the correct time
• I am insufficient
 • I am too old/young

Don't allow your excuses to hold you back any longer!

4. Lack of Confidence

Lack of confidence in yourself or your ability to achieve your goals will inevitably hold you back. Our actions, or lack thereof, are influenced by what goes on in our subconscious mind. We have self-limiting and negative beliefs that may be preventing us from enjoying an extraordinary life.

Nothing will be able to stop you if you believe in yourself. Bringing your limiting beliefs into focus will help you achieve your objectives.
Don't let your lack of confidence keep you back!

5. There Isn't A Big Picture

Others refer to what I call a breakthrough goal as a BHAG - Big Hairy Audacious Goal. A goal is what you need to keep you motivated and drive you to achieve it every day. Start small and dream big. You'll need a strong enough passion to propel you forward. Your ambitions will not motivate you until you first dream big.

For your objectives to be beneficial to you, they must assist you in realizing your ambitions. Those lofty ambitions. Goals can only motivate you, help you stay focused, and help you make the adjustments you need to make, as well as provide you the fortitude to overcome difficulties as you chase your big-picture dreams if they matter to you.

Stop allowing your big picture to stifle your progress!

6. Inability To Concentrate

Your chances of success are slashed every moment you lose focus. When we spread our focus too thin, we dilute our effort and lose the ability to focus on the most significant tasks. When you're pulled in a lot of different directions and have a lot of conflicting priorities fighting for your attention, it's easy to lose track of what's important. Any attempts to achieve vital goals will be harmed as a result of this.

Stop allowing your lack of concentration to keep you back!

7. Failure to Make a Plan

Finally, if you don't have a strategy, it's easy to become lost along the route. Consider driving across the country without a map, say from London to Glasgow. While you have a rough route in mind, there are many lands to cover and a lot of false turns and dead ends to be avoided. You can get there with the help of a GPS. It plots your path and creates a plan for you. A plan provides you with the road map you need to reach your objectives. This is the process of determining what you need to accomplish to reach your objectives. This is where you put in the time and effort to write out a plan of the steps you need to follow, the resources you'll need, and the amount of time you'll need to invest.

Stop allowing the lack of a strategy holds you back!

8. Not Keeping Track of Your Progress and Making Necessary Modifications

Goals, by their very nature, take time to attain. Therefore, it's critical to keep track of your progress. You won't know what's working and what's not if you don't get quick and actionable feedback. You won't be able to tell when to alter or when to keep doing what you're doing. Anyone who is continuously successful in accomplishing their goals also reviews their goals and progress regularly. Regularly reviewing your goals allows you to make early modifications to stay on track.

Stop allowing not reviewing and adjusting your progress to hold you back!

CPSIA information can be obtained
at www.ICGtesting.com
Printed in the USA
LVHW012053101022
730380LV00013B/592